HATS
for
BRIDES & WEDDINGS

Pear shaped bridal cap trimmed with a tulle ruffle

HATS
for
BRIDES & WEDDINGS

Margo-Ann Daly

Kangaroo Press

Acknowledgments
Many thanks to those who helped in the creation of this book. A special thanks to Steve Norris of Wentworth Falls for his photography and patience. Also thanks to Vicky and Michelle of Wentworth Falls and Kate Trevillion of Nowra. To my husband Phil for his patience and organisation. Lastly to my mum Gloria who gave me that added push to get this book on its way.

First published in 1992 by Kangaroo Press Pty Ltd
3 Whitehall Road (P.O. Box 75) Kenthurst 2156
Typeset by G.T. Setters Pty Limited
Printed in Hong Kong by Colorcraft Ltd

ISBN 0 086417 459 4

Contents

Satin-bound crinoline bridal hat (page 35)

Introduction

This book has not been written to change the traditional techniques of millinery, but with today's busy lifestyle shortcuts are often invaluable. In any case, bridal millinery is an easy craft to learn, particularly for those who are already familiar with other crafts, and it is also closely linked with floral art, especially bridal headpieces. The techniques involved are very versatile, and the basics explained here are also relevant to hats of a less formal nature.

Bridal millinery is influenced by fashion like any other form of apparel, and hats and headpieces are often made to suit a particular gown or face. But the basic techniques remain the same. Variety is achieved by altering size and shape, and particularly by the use of fabrics and trimmings. Once the basic techniques have been mastered, your imagination is the only limiting factor.

1 Covering the Basic Hat Shapes

Covering a hat shape gives you the opportunity to create your own unique model in fabrics matching your outfit. For beginners or those who like shortcuts ready-made shapes are available (see list of suppliers); the more adventurous or experienced can try making their own (see page 63).

Equipment
Plate 1

1. Hat shapes
2. Fabric
3. Wadding or wool felt
4. Glue
5. Needle and cotton
6. Dressmaker's pins
7. Tape measure
8. Iron
9. Scissors
10. Pressing cloth

Points to Remember

1. Always have clean hands when starting to cover a hat, especially for white and pale colours.
2. Cut your fabric on the bias (cross), as this will give maximum stretch.
3. Do not add too much glue at any one time, as it can be difficult to handle at first.
4. To remove any excess glue from fabric use nail polish remover.
5. Always cut bias strips before other pattern pieces.

Pear Shape Cocktail Hat
Plate 4

Materials
Pear hat shape
Wadding 20 × 20 cm (8″ × 8″)
50 cm (20″) fabric
50 cm (20″) of 1 cm (⅜″) wide lace
White lining fabric
Veiling (optional)
Comb
Craft glue

Method

1. Apply glue over the top of the shape, then place wadding over it and press down. Cut off excess wadding.
2. Cut a piece of fabric 20 × 25 cm (8″ × 10″), place it over the shape and pin back, front and sides, stretching the fabric as you go.
3.. Turn the shape over and apply glue about 1 cm (⅜″) from the wired edge. Allow the glue to become tacky. See diagram 1.
4. Then pull the fabric over the wire edge and glue down, pulling the fabric with the left hand and pressing it down with the right thumb, making sure there are no wrinkles on the right side. When the glue is fairly dry cut away excess fabric. See diagram 2.
5. Cut a bias strip 50 × 10 cm (20″ × 4″) and fold in half lengthways. Place the end of the folded band at the back of the shape allowing 3 cm (1¼″) for turning under and pin in place.
6. Stretch the band around the shape making sure it is lying flat with 2.5 cm (1″) of fabric on the right side of the shape. Pin in place. See diagrams 3 and 4.

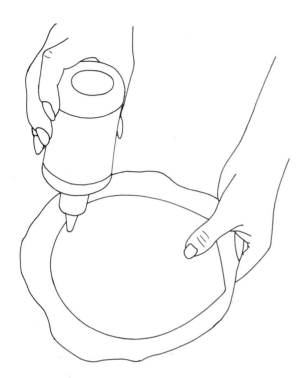

Diagram 1

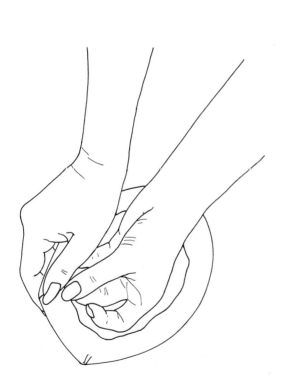

Diagram 3

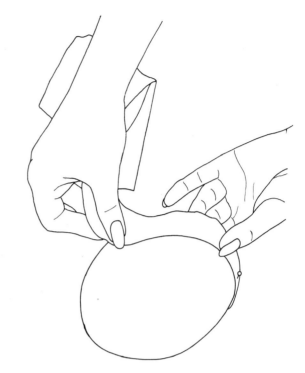

Diagram 2

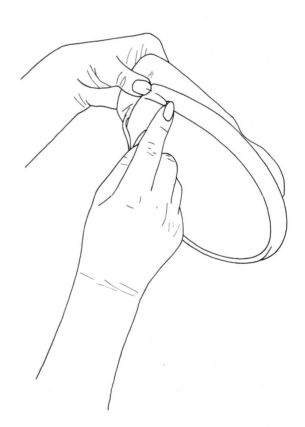

Diagram 4

7. Turn the shape over, apply glue around the edge and glue the fabric down. As there is a double layer of fabric more glue might be needed to secure both layers. Turn the ends under the inside of the shape and glue down. See diagrams 5 and 6.

8. Apply the veiling next. See instructions on page 61.
9. Cut the lining fabric about 1 cm (⅜'') smaller than the shape to fit inside and cover the raw edges. Turn the hat over, apply a line of glue along the raw edges, then insert the lining and press it in place. The lining might need to be cut slightly. See diagrams 7 and 8.

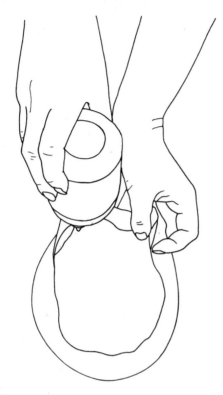

Diagram 5

Diagram 7

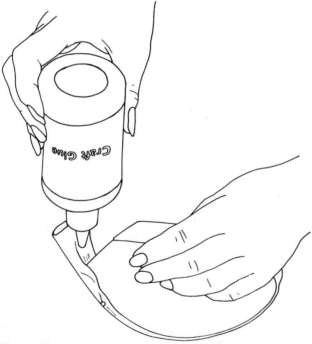

Diagram 6

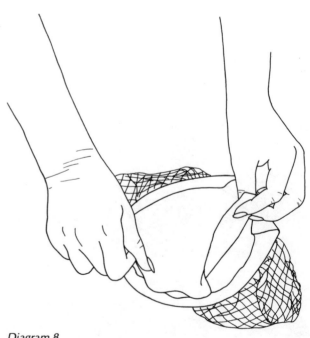

Diagram 8

10. To cover the raw edge of the lining apply a line of glue along the edges and cover this with lace. See diagrams 9 and 10.

11. Apply a line of glue along the edge of the comb and let it get tacky. Place the comb at the back of the hat with the teeth of the comb facing the outside of the hat, then press down and hold for a few minutes. See diagram 11.

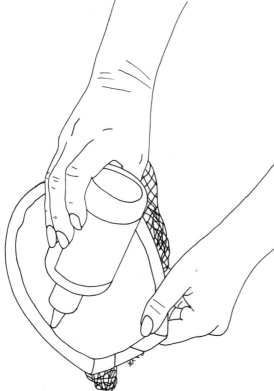

Diagram 9

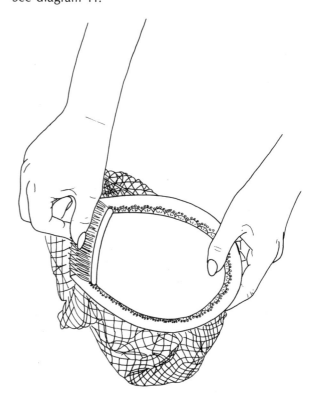

Diagram 11

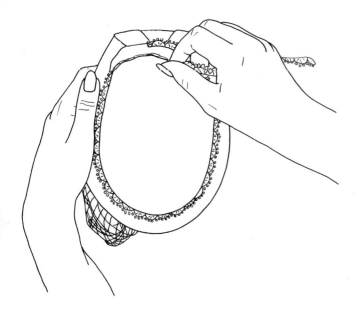

Diagram 10

Pearl Shape Cocktail Hat

Plate 3

Materials

Pearl hat shape (tear drop shape)
Wadding 20 × 20 cm (8″ × 8″)
50 cm (20″) fabric
White lining fabric
50 cm (20″) of 1 cm (⅜″) wide lace
1 metre (39″) of veiling (optional)
Comb
Craft glue

Method

1. For covering, follow the instructions for the pear hat shape.
2. Make a bias band 50 × 10 cm (20″ × 4″) and fold in half lengthways. Place the end of the band at the front of the hat, overlapping the front edge of the shape 3 cm (1¼″) and pin in place. See diagram 1.

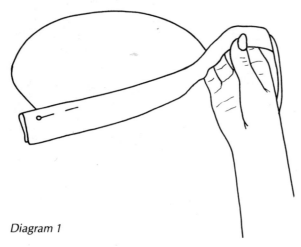

Diagram 1

3. Stretch the band along the wired edge until you return to the front, overlapping 3 cm (1¼″). Pin to secure. See diagram 2.

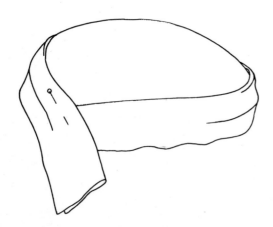

Diagram 2

4. Turn the shape over, apply glue around the inside edge and glue the fabric down, including the ends at the front. See diagrams 3 and 4. Trim off any excess fabric.

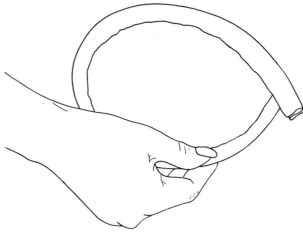

Diagram 3

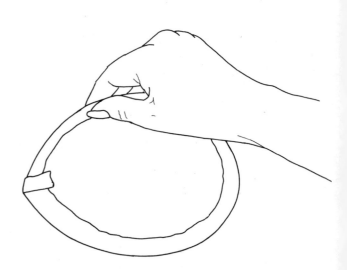

Diagram 4

5. Next apply the veiling, followed by the lining and comb. (See pear shape.)

Pill Box Cocktail Hat

Plate 5

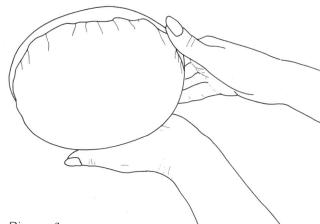

Materials

Pill box hat shape 5 cm (2'') deep
1 metre (39'') fabric
Wadding 20 × 20 cm (8'' × 8'')
1 metre (39'') of 2 cm (¾'') wide lace
Hat veiling (optional)
Comb
Craft glue

Method

1. To cover the hat apply a small amount of glue to the top of the hat shape. Place wadding over it and press down. Trim away excess wadding.
2. Cut a circle of fabric 20 cm (8'') in diameter. Apply a bead of glue around the side of the hat about 2.5 cm (1'') down from the top and allow it to go tacky. Place fabric over the top of the shape, stretching and glueing down. See diagrams 1 and 2.

Diagram 2

3. Make two bias strips to fit around the shape, both 8 cm (3'') wide. If your shape is more or less than 5 cm (2'') deep you may need to vary this.
4. Fold the first bias strip in half lengthways and position it around the hat, starting at the back with a pin to hold and stretching as you go. Keep the folded edge level with the top edge of the hat. Then pin in place at the back. See diagrams 3 and 4.

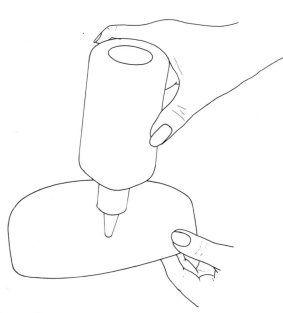

Diagram 1

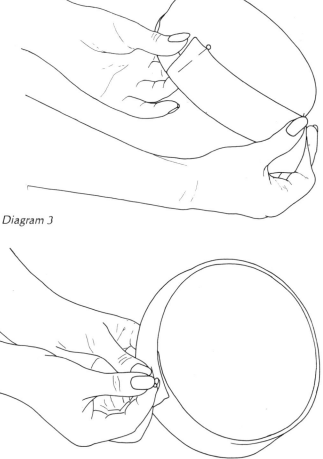

Diagram 3

Diagram 4

5. Repeat this with the second bias strip, starting 2.5 cm (1'') down from the top with the fold sitting more or less in the middle of the band. Pin to hold at the back. See diagrams 5 and 6.

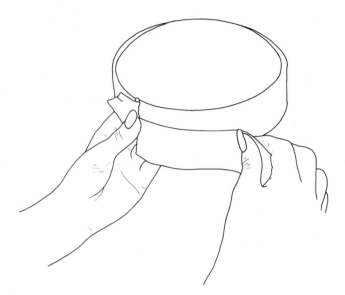

Diagram 5

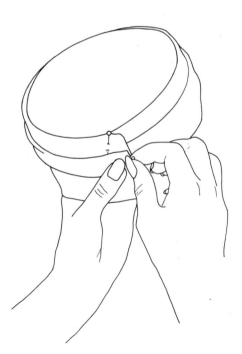

Diagram 6

6. Trim off any excess fabric at the back, tack to secure and remove pins. See diagram 7.

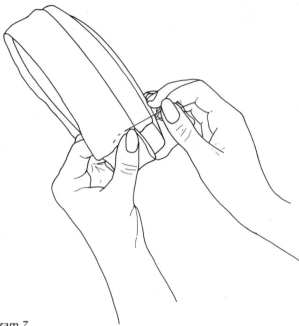

Diagram 7

7. To finish the back and tidy up the raw edges cut a small piece of fabric 8 × 4 cm (3'' × 1½''). Fold in the edges so it measures 6 × 2 cm (2½'' × ¾'') and press with an iron.
8. Wrong side out, place the end of the strip of fabric under the top of the bias strips at the back of the hat, with the remaining fabric going towards the front of the hat. Stitch or glue the covered end in place. See diagram 8.

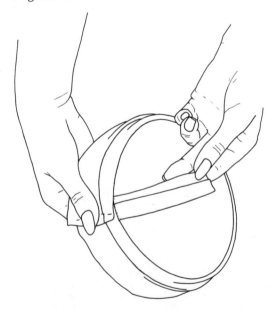

Diagram 8

9. Now bring the fabric strip back over to cover the stitching and raw edges. See diagram 9. (If the strip of fabric doesn't lie flat to the band, place a little glue under it and press down.)

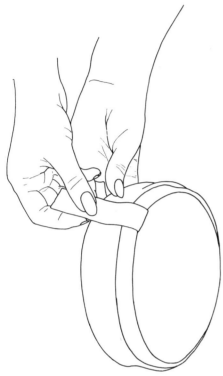

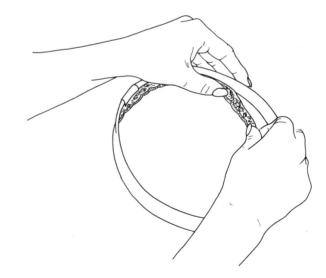

Diagram 10

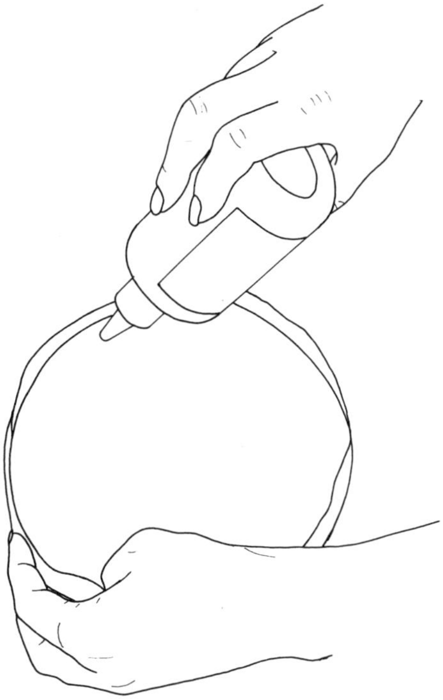

Diagram 9

10. Place glue inside the hat just below the wired edge, fold fabric and fabric strip over the wired edge and glue down. See diagram 10. (As there is a double layer of fabric more glue might be needed to secure both layers.)
11. To tidy up the raw edges inside the hat apply a line of glue along the raw edge and position lace right around the inside, starting at the back. See diagram 11.
12. Apply a bow or other desired trim.

Diagram 11

Satin-Covered Brim Hat

Plate 10

Materials
Shallow crown shape and brim shape
2 metres (2¼ yds) white bias satin
Flower spray
60 cm (24″) of 2 cm (¾″) wide lace
1 metre (39″) poly satin
60 cm (24″) of 5 mm wide fused pearls
Comb
Craft glue

Method
1. To cover the crown, cut a piece of fabric 25 × 25 cm (10″ × 10″), and apply a bead of glue around the wired edge of the crown. See diagram 1.

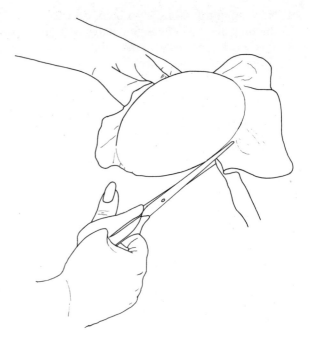

Diagram 2

3. To cover the brim, cut two circles of fabric slightly bigger than the brim. Apply a line of glue around the wired edge and around the tabs. See diagrams 3 and 4.

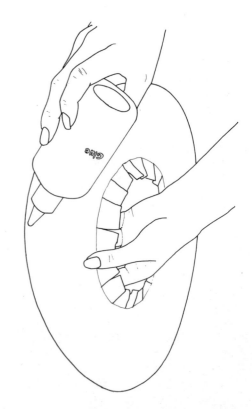

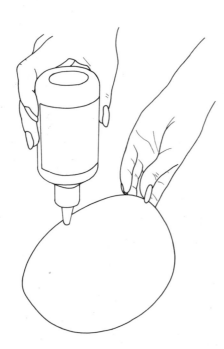

Diagram 1

2. Place the fabric over the crown and pin in place at front, back and sides, stretching as you go. Now glue the fabric down, keeping it stretched. There will probably be a few wrinkles: remove them as best you can. These will, however, be covered by the band. When dry, trim away excess fabric. See diagram 2.

Diagram 3

Plate 1: Equipment for covering hats (page 8)

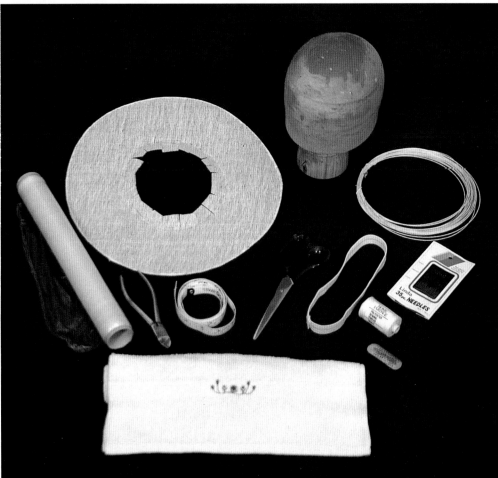

Plate 2: Equipment for blocking your own shapes (page 63)

Plate 3: Pearl shape cocktail hat (page 12)

Plate 5: Pill box cocktail hat (page 13)

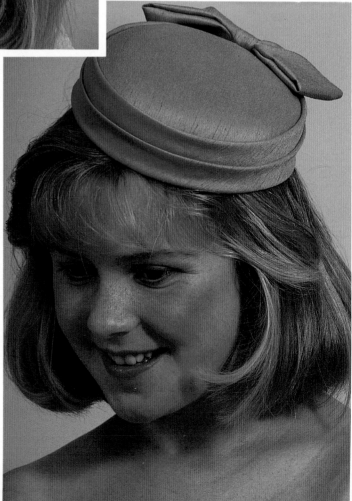

Plate 4: Pear shape cocktail hat (page 8)

18

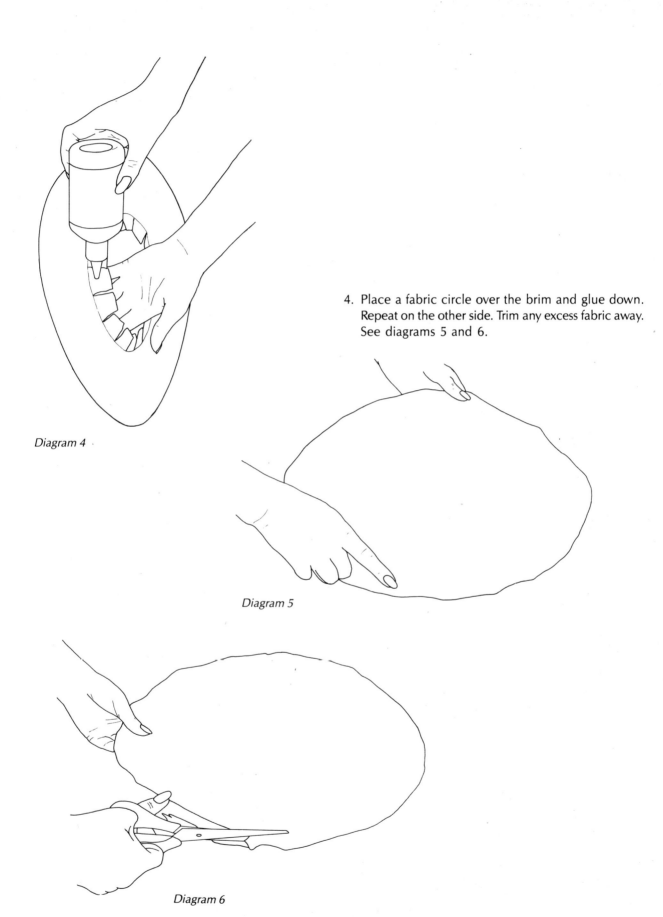

Diagram 4

4. Place a fabric circle over the brim and glue down. Repeat on the other side. Trim any excess fabric away. See diagrams 5 and 6.

Diagram 5

Diagram 6

5. To apply the satin bias, first iron it lengthways to make an edge down the centre. Apply a line of glue along the wired edge of the brim. Lay the satin bias against the edge, stretching slightly as you go around. Tidy up the join by folding over one end of the bias and glueing it down. Apply more glue if necessary. See diagram 7.

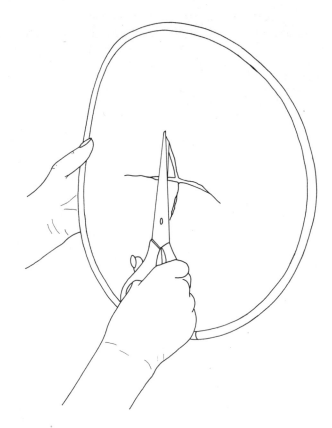

Diagram 8

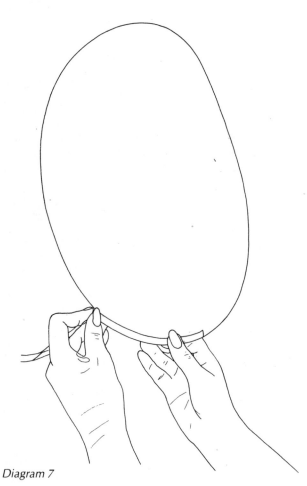

Diagram 7

6. To finish off the brim, cut the fabric in the middle by snipping it slightly, then cutting it in four places, then eight, or to correspond with the tabs on the original brim. See diagrams 8 and 9.

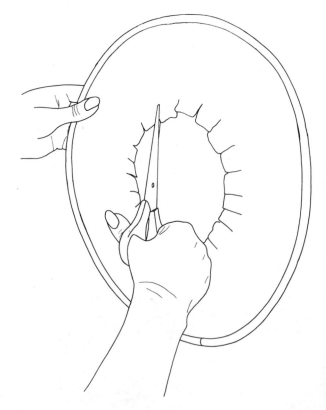

Diagram 9

7. Place the crown over the brim and pin the front, back and sides to the collar. Sew together. See diagrams 10 and 11.

8. Apply the satin bias band, pin it to the back of the crown and stretch it as you go around the crown. Glue it in place. If you like, you can add an additional row of overlapping bias band for effect. See diagram 12.

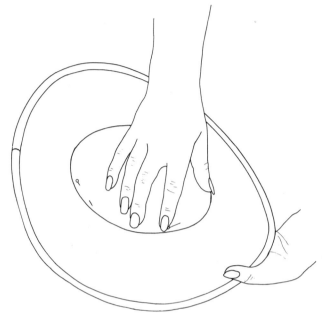

Diagram 10

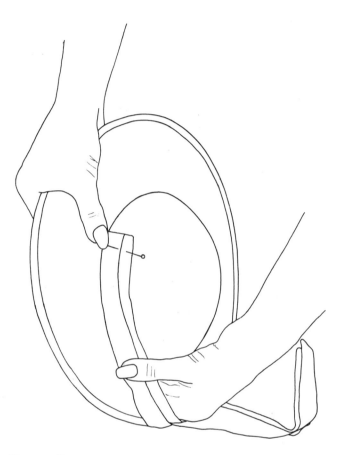

Diagram 12

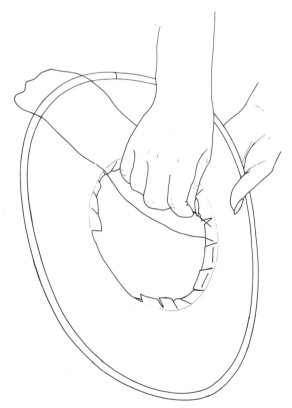

Diagram 11

9. Apply a line of glue just below the band and glue a row of pearls around the base of the crown.
10. To tidy up the inside head fitting, apply a line of glue and position the lace over it (instructions as for pill box hat).
11. Apply a tulle bow or ruffle and the flower spray.

2 Creating Beautiful Bridal Hats

Satin and Pearl Pear Shape

Plate 7

Materials
Pear shape hat
Wadding
2.4 metres (2¾ yds) of 2 mm fused pearls
25 cm (10″) fabric
50 cm (20″) of 1 cm (⅜″) lace
Lining fabric
Comb
Craft glue

Method
1. Follow the instructions for covering the pear hat shape, omitting the band. Bind the edge with satin bias instead.
2. First make four strands of pearls by cutting the original length into 60 cm (24″) sections. Sew these together at one end or tape them with white florist's tape.
3. Apply a fairly liberal line of glue around the edge of the hat and let it get very tacky. Starting at the back, hold the four rows of pearls to the glue and twist them over each other, pressing them down into the bed of glue as you proceed around the edge of the hat. Cut away any excess pearls. See diagrams 1 and 2.

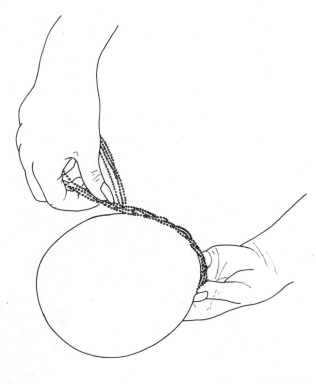

Diagram 1

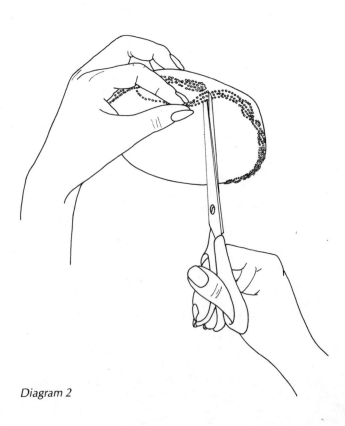

Diagram 2

Satin Leaves and Flower Spray

Plate 7

Materials

7 satin leaves
3 medium flowers
2 small flowers
1 bunch of pearl sprays
Florist's tape

Method

1. Tape one spray of pearls to each satin leaf.
2. There are two flower sprays each side of the hat. The first spray is made up of 4 satin leaves and 3 flowers. Tape one medium flower to one satin leaf, then tape two satin leaves and a small flower together, ending with a satin leaf and a medium flower. See diagram 1.
3. The second spray is made up of 3 satin leaves and 2 flowers. Tape a satin leaf to a medium flower, followed by two satin leaves and a small flower. See diagram 2.
4. Tidy up the ends of the two sprays and sew them to the back of the hat. Add a tulle ruffle, then the lining and comb. See diagram 3.

Diagram 1

Diagram 2

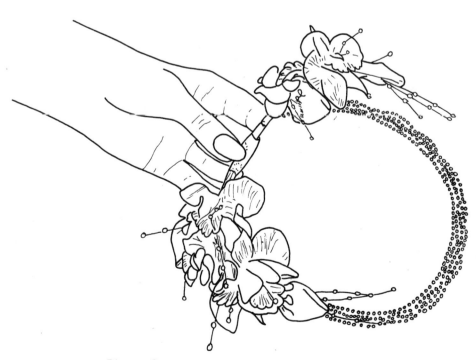

Diagram 3

23

Lace-Covered Pearl Shape

Plate 8

Materials

Pearl hat shape (tear drop shape)
Wadding
50 cm (20'') of fused pearls (5 mm wide)
25 cm (10'') fabric
20 × 20 cm (8'' × 8'') lace fabric
Lining fabric
60 cm (24'') of 1 cm (¼'') lace
Comb
Craft glue

Method

1. Follow the instructions for covering the basic pearl shape, omitting the band.
2. Apply a line of glue around the edge of the hat and place the lace fabric over it, stretching slightly. When the lace is secure and fairly dry, trim away the excess. See diagrams 1 and 2.

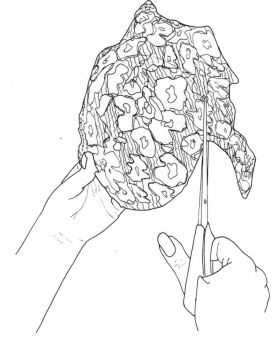

Diagram 2

3. Apply the band according to the previous instructions for the basic pearl shape.
4. Apply a line of glue around the hat directly above the band and fix the beads in place. See diagrams 3 and 4.
5. Add trim, lining and comb.

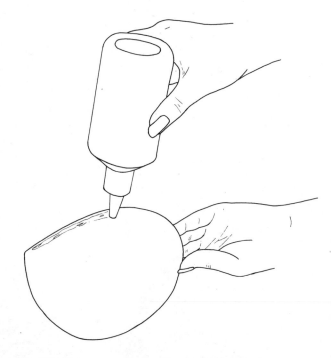

Diagram 1

Diagram 3

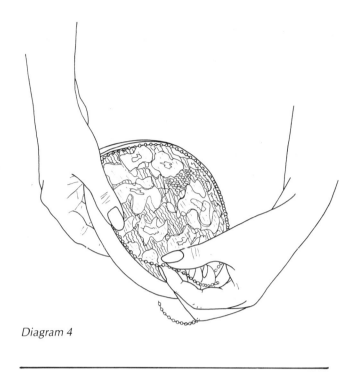

Diagram 4

Lace and Pearl Pill Box

Plate 9

Materials
Pill box shape
Wadding (optional)
50 cm (20″) poly satin fabric
20 × 20 cm (8″ × 8″) lace fabric
60 cm (24″) of 2 cm (¾″) lace
50 cm (20″) of fused pearls (5 mm wide)
Fabric flowers and buds
Comb
Craft glue

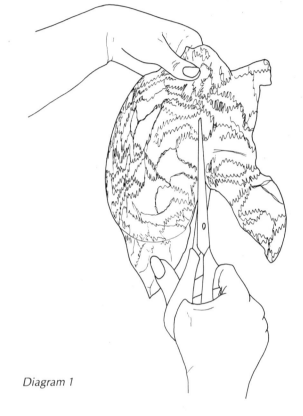

Diagram 1

Method
1. Follow the instructions for the pill box hat, omitting the band.
2. Apply a line of glue 2.5 cm (1″) down from the top around the side. Place the lace fabric over the top and glue down. When fairly dry, trim away excess lace. See diagram 1.
3. Apply the band as for the basic pill box shape.
4. Apply a line of glue on top of the hat around the edge right next to the band, and glue the pearls in place (refer to the lace-covered pearl shape).
5. Add the fabric flowers, sewing on each flower and bud separately. Bind the buds first with white florist's tape, then with cream tulle, as this helps to blend them in with the fabric. See diagram 2.
6. Finish off the inside of the hat with lace and a comb.

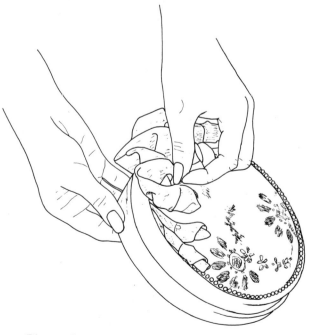

Diagram 2

Lace and Satin Bridal Hat

Plate 6

Materials

Crown and brim shape
2 metres (2¼ yds) white bias satin
Flower spray
1 metre (39″) poly satin
125 cm (50″) of 12 cm (5″) wide lace
60 cm (24″) of 2 cm (¾″) wide lace
60 cm (24″) fused pearls (5 mm)
Needle and cotton
Craft glue
Comb

Method

1. Follow the instructions for the satin-covered brim hat.
2. Before sewing the crown to the brim, gather or pleat the lace slightly. Starting at the back pin the lace to the brim collar, leaving a 2 cm (¾″) overlap at the brim edge. Sew the lace to the brim collar. See diagram.
3. Glue or sew the crown to the brim, and add the band, pearls and tulle bow according to the instructions for the satin-covered brim hat.
4. Cut out lace flowers from the remaining lace and glue these to the crown, adding pearls and sequins if desired.
5. Finish off the inside of the hat with lace and a comb.

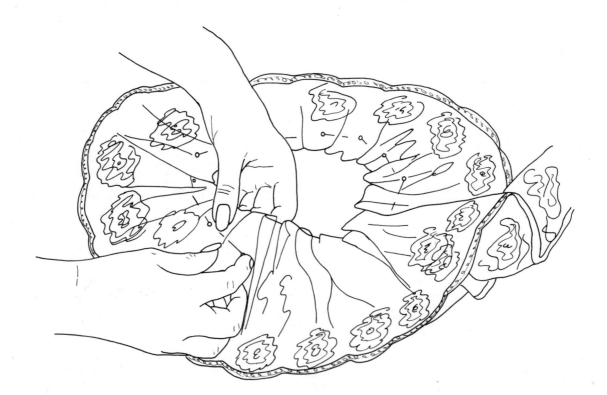

Plate 6: Lace and satin bridal hat (opposite)

Plate 7: Satin and pearl pear shape bridal hat (page 22)

Plate 9: Lace and pearl pill box bridal hat (page 25)

Plate 8: Lace-covered pearl shape bridal hat (page 24)

28

*Plate 10: Satin-
covered brim hat
(page 16)*

Lace Appliquéd Crinoline Bridal Hat *Plate 11*

Materials
White crinoline hat
12 to 15 appliqué flowers
1 metre (39") millinery wire
2.5 metres (2¾ yds) white bias satin
Needle and cotton
Spray of flowers (optional)
Comb
Craft glue

Method
1. Wire the brim edge with millinery wire, either by hand using blanket stitch or with a wide zigzag stitch on a machine.
2. Bind the wire edge with the satin bias, following the instructions for the satin-covered brim hat.
3. Apply the satin band around the crown. Sew or glue in place.
4. Arrange the appliqués around the hat. When you have the flowers organised, apply a small amount of glue to each and glue them in place. As glue doesn't adhere very well to the crinoline, sewing them in about four spots will give extra support. See diagram.
5. Finish off by adding a tulle bow or ruffle and a comb.

3 Romantic Bridal Headpieces

Flower and Pearl V-Shaped Headpiece *Plate 12*

Materials
6 medium flowers
140 5 mm single pearls
1 pearl drop (optional)
1 metre (39'') millinery wire
6 pearl sprays (3 per spray)
White florist's tape
Tulle ruffle
50 cm (20'') of 1 cm (3/8'') tulle
Comb

Method
1. Remove the paper wrapping from the millinery wire. Cut the wire into two lengths, one 60 cm (24''), the other 40 cm (16'').
2. With the longer length of wire thread 35 pearls, then the pearl drop, then another 35 pearls. Make the wire into a circle and tape at the back, overlapping 5 cm (2''). Tape down to the pearls to stop them moving. See diagram 1.
3. Thread the remaining 70 pearls on to the smaller length of wire. Tape this to the wire circle. See diagram 2.

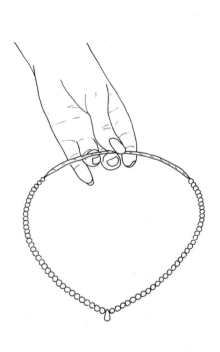

Diagram 1

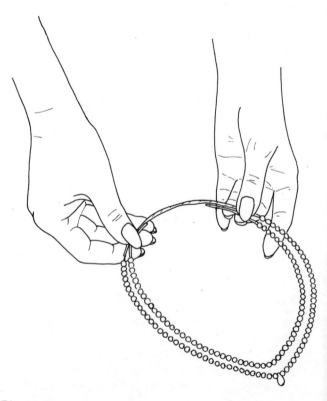

Diagram 2

4. Bend the pearl band to form a V shape.
5. To make flower sprays tape a spray of pearls to each flower. Arrange three flowers to form a triangle. Make two sprays, one each side, then tape the flowers to both sides just above the pearls. See diagram 3.

6. There should be about 15 cm (6'') left at the back for the ruffle. Wrap tulle around the back section until it is fairly neat and of even width (this helps to secure the ruffle).
7. Finish off by attaching the comb first, tying it to the back of the headpiece with fine covered wire. See diagram 4. Lastly, attach the ruffle. See diagram 4.

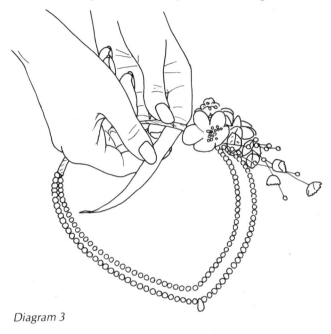

Diagram 3

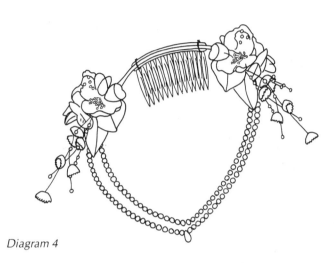

Diagram 4

Fabric Flower and Pearl Circlet   *Plate 13*

Materials
15 fabric flowers, 5 × 5 cm (2'' × 2'')
60 cm (24'') millinery wire
White florist's tape
Dried baby's breath
Ruffle
1 metre (39'') of 1 cm (⅜'') wide tulle
Comb

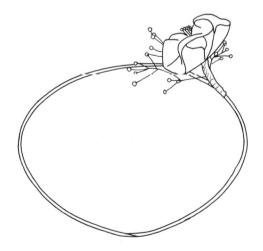

Method
1. Make the fabric flowers following the instructions under trimmings (page 57).
2. Bend the millinery wire into a circle of the right head size, overlapping the ends 5 cm (2'').
3. Starting at the back and leaving about 12 cm (5'') for the ruffle, lay a fabric flower against the wire and tape. Tape a small amount of baby's breath each side of the flower, then apply the next flower and add more baby's breath, repeating until you reach the other side of the ruffle space. See diagram.

4. Wrap the back of the circle with tulle, then add the comb and ruffle.

Pearl and Sequin Headpiece

Plate 14

Materials

28 pre-made sequin leaves:
  8 large net leaves or millinery leaves
  4 medium leaves
  16 small leaves
2 bunches of pearl sprays (12 sprays per bunch)
White florist's tape
20 cm (8'') millinery wire
Comb

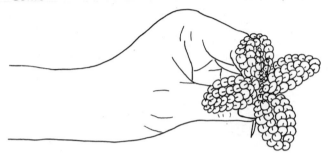

Diagram 1

Method

1. Make the sequin leaves following the instructions under trimmings (page 57).
2. Tape three pearl sprays to each of the large sequin leaves.
3. Make a four-petalled flower out of the small sequin leaves by taping them together with a pearl spray in the centre. Make four of these. See diagram 1.
4. Make one four-petalled flower out of medium sequin leaves, taping them together and adding a pearl spray in the middle.
5. Tape the leaves and flowers to the millinery wire, starting at the ends and working towards the middle.
6. Firstly, tape three leaves to one end, then two small flowers, the large flower and one side leaf. Next, starting at the opposite end, tape three leaves, two small flowers and one side leaf. See diagram 2.
7. Finish off by adding the comb.

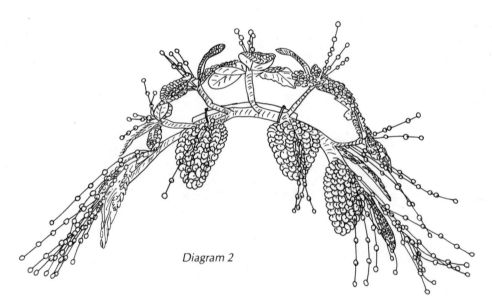

Diagram 2

4 Advanced Designs

Satin-Bound Crinoline Bridal Hat *Plates 15, 16*

Materials
Small shallow crown shape
Satin fabric 25 × 25 cm (10″ × 10″)
1.5 metres (1¾ yds) satin bias
1 metre (39″) white crinoline
1 metre (39″) of 4 mm fused pearls
Appliqué flowers
Lining fabric
50 cm (20″) of 1 cm (⅜″) wide lace
Needle and cotton
Spray of flowers
Comb
Glue

Method
1. Cover the crown shape with fabric, then bind the edge with satin bias.
2. Gather the crinoline until it forms a circle, easing the gather evenly all around until it sits flat. (The object is to have the inner circle slightly smaller than the crown shape.) See diagram 1.

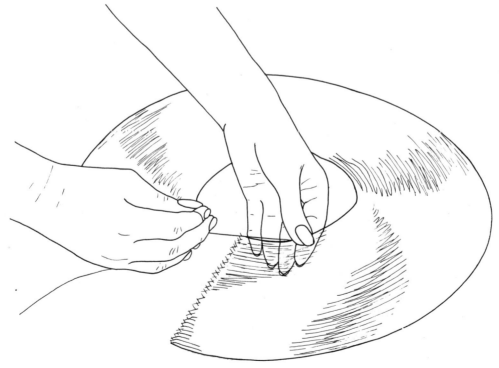

Diagram 1

3. Turn the shape over and place the crinoline around the inside edge and pin front, sides and back. Sew the crinoline to the satin edge with whip stitch. See diagram 2.

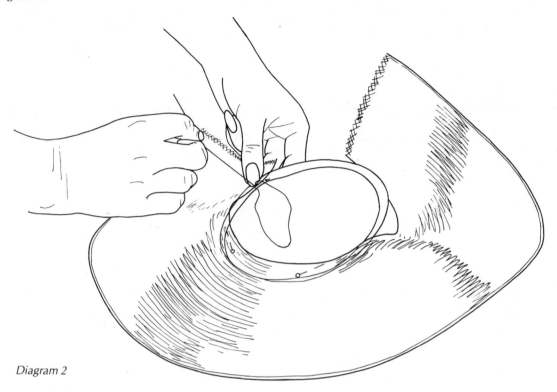

Diagram 2

4. Wire the outer edge with millinery wire. Run glue around the wired edge and apply the bias satin.
5. Take the two ends of covered wire at the back of the hat, overlapping them, and place them under the crown, pinning to secure. Sew the wire very securely with stab stitch. Any stitches on the right side of the hat will be covered by the pearls and lace ruffle. See diagrams 3 and 4. Clip away any excess covered wire.

Diagram 3

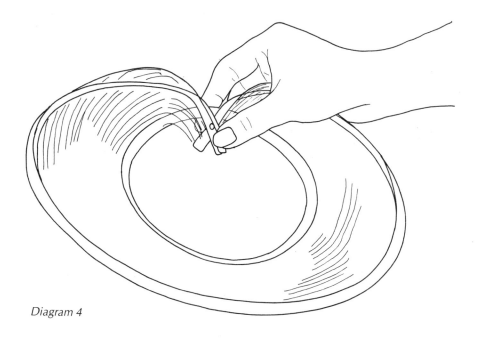

Diagram 4

6. To finish off the hat, glue a few appliqué flowers to the crown and two or three rows of pearls around the edge of the crown.

7. Affix the ruffle and flower spray, and lastly the lining and comb.

Pleated Satin and Diamanté Bridal Hat

Plate 17

Materials
Shallow crown shape
Brim shape
1 metre (39'') satin
50 cm (20'') satin bias
75 cm (30'') of diamantés or pearls
Lining fabric
50 cm (20'') of 1 cm (⅜'') wide lace
Craft glue
Wadding
Comb

Method
1. Cover the crown shape with fabric, then bind the edge with satin bias.
2. To cover the brim, lay it on the fabric and measure out twice the width of the brim from the centre tabs, plus an extra 2 cm (¾''). See diagram 1.

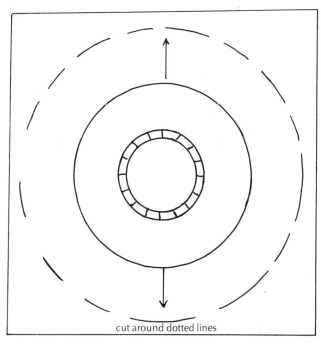

cut around dotted lines

Diagram 1

3. Leaving the brim on the circle of fabric, gather around the edge of the fabric with needle and cotton. Pull tight to bring the gathers into the middle. See diagrams 2 and 3.

4. Organise the gathers so they are not too thick in one spot, pin the gathered fabric to the collar of the brim, and tack in place. See diagram 4.

5. Turn brim over and cut out the fabric in the centre. Glue the fabric to the collar or tabs. See instructions for satin brim hat (page 20).

6. Glue the crown to the brim.

7. Finish off the hat by glueing the diamantés or pearls to the crown and adding the bow and ruffle. (Notice the bow has diamantés wrapped around the middle instead of fabric.) See plate 17.

8. Add the lining and comb.

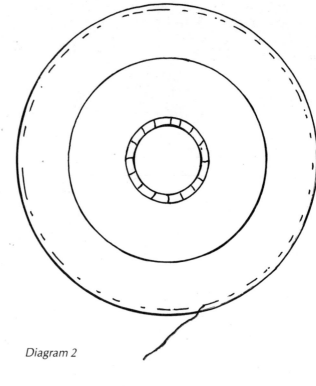

Diagram 2

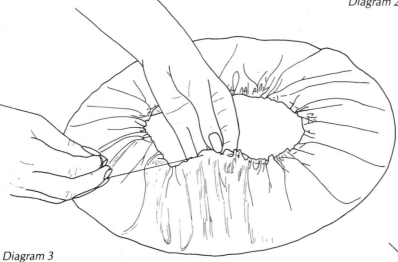

Diagram 3

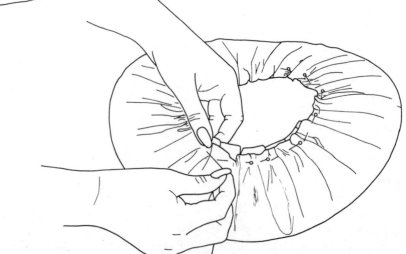

Diagram 4

Plate 12: Flower and pearl V-shaped headpiece (page 32)

Plate 14: Pearl and sequin headpiece (page 34)

Plate 13: Fabric flower and pearl circlet (page 33)

Plate 15: Satin-bound crinoline bridal hat with veil attached (page 35)

Plate 16: Another version of the satin-bound crinoline bridal hat in cream (page 35)

Plate 17: Pleated satin and diamanté bridal hat (page 37)

Plate 18: Two-tiered V-shape bridal hat (page 43)

Plate 19: Shoulder-length veil (page 44)

Two-Tiered V-Shaped Bridal Hat

Plate 18

Materials

Pearl hat shape
25 cm (10'') fabric
Wadding
Appliqué flowers
50 cm (20'') satin bias
42 cm (16½'') millinery wire
60 cm (24'') satin tube ribbon (rouleau)
2 metres (2¼ yds) of fused 3 mm wide half pearls
Lining fabric
50 cm (20'') of 1 cm (¾'') lace
Craft glue
Comb

Method

1. Cover the hat shape, then bind the edge with satin bias.
2. Cut the wire into two pieces, 20 cm (8'') and 22 cm (9'') long. Thread the tube ribbon (rouleau) onto the wire and bend to form a V shape.
3. Glue these two sections underneath the sides of the hat, about 9 cm (3½'') from the front point of the hat shape. See diagram 1.

4. Apply glue around the outside edge of the hat at the back and sides only, as well as along the longer rouleau piece, and glue the pearls down. See diagram 2. Apply another row of glue just above the previous row, right around the edge of the hat, and glue the pearls in place. See diagram 3. Apply glue to the middle rouleau and glue the pearls in place.

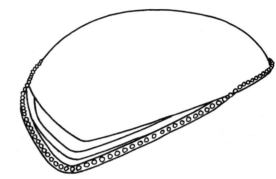

Diagram 2

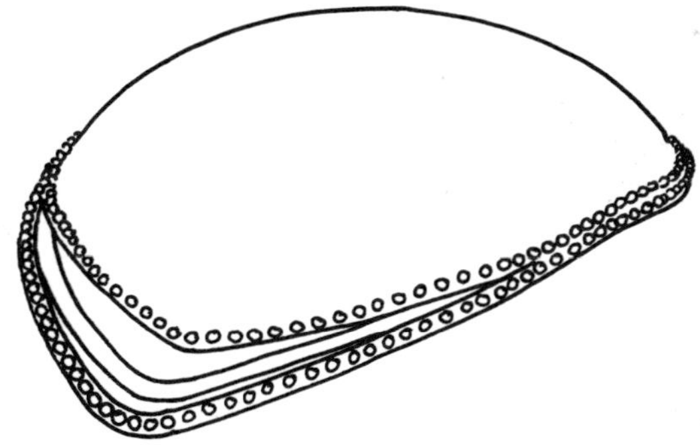

Diagram 3

5. Finish off by affixing appliqué flowers to the top of the hat. Add the trim, lining and comb.

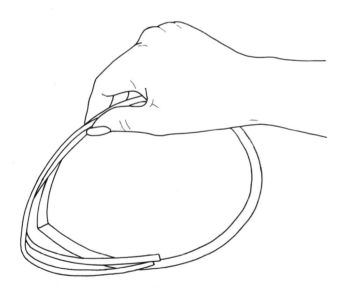

Diagram 1

5 Bridal Veils

Fluted Veil and Ruffle

Materials
Tulle
Fishing line (monofilament), 7 kg (15 lb)
Sewing machine

Method
1. Fluting the edge of a veil is basically a matter of trial and error, depending on your sewing skills and patience.

2. If your machine has automatic tension set it for fine fabric. If you have a basic zigzag machine, set the tension about halfway. Now set the zigzag stitch on its widest setting, but not too long, about midway, and place the fishing line inside the tulle, overlapping 1 cm (⅜''). Position this under the sewing foot, bring the needle down into the tulle and start to sew.

Shoulder-Length Veil   Plate 19

Materials
1.5 metres (1¾ yds) white tulle
6 metres (7 yds) fishing line, 7 kg (15 lb)

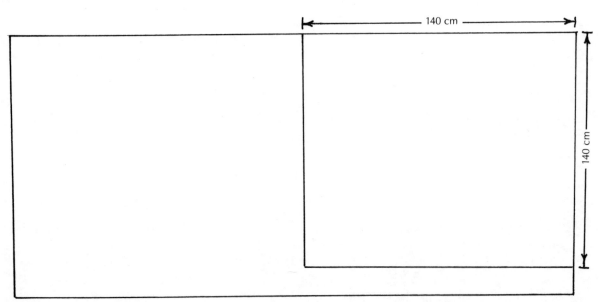

140 cm

140 cm

Diagram 1

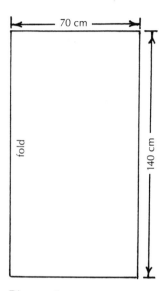

Diagram 2

Method

1. Lay the tulle out on a flat surface—width of tulle is usually 270 cm (106''). Measure out a square with sides 140 cm (55''), pin and cut out. See diagram 1 on previous page.
2. Fold tulle from left to right so it measures 70 × 140 cm (28'' × 55''). See diagram 2. Then fold again from top to bottom so it measures 70 × 70 cm (28'' × 28''). The folds must be on top and on the left side. Now curve the corner as in diagram 3.
3. Now fold the tulle as in diagram 4 and gather the centre 40 cm (16'') of the fold line to a width of 9 cm (3½'').

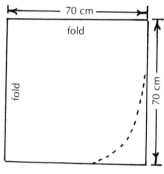

Diagram 3

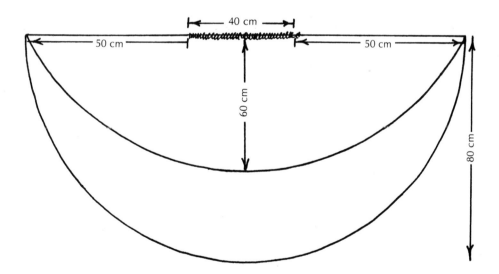

Diagram 4

Finger-Tip Veil

Plate 20

Materials

2 metres (2¼ yds) tulle
8 metres (9 yds) of fishing line/lace

Method

1. Follow the basic instructions for the shoulder-length veil. Measure the tulle to 180 × 90 cm (71″ × 36″), then fold it to measure 90 × 90 cm (36″ × 36″), and curve the corner. See diagrams 1 and 2.
2. Now fold the veil as in diagram 3 and gather the centre 60 cm (24″) of the fold line to 9 cm (3½″).

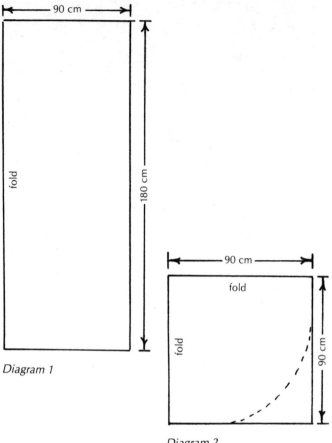

Diagram 1

Diagram 2

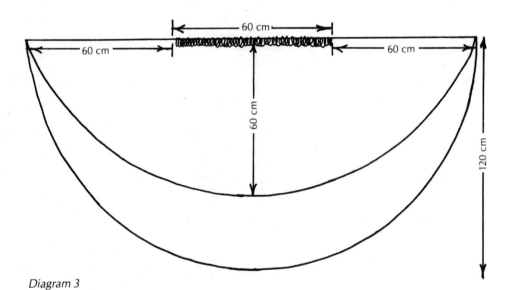

Diagram 3

Plate 20: Finger-tip veil (opposite)

Plate 21: Three-tiered veil (page 51)

Plate 22: Cathedral-length veil (page 52)

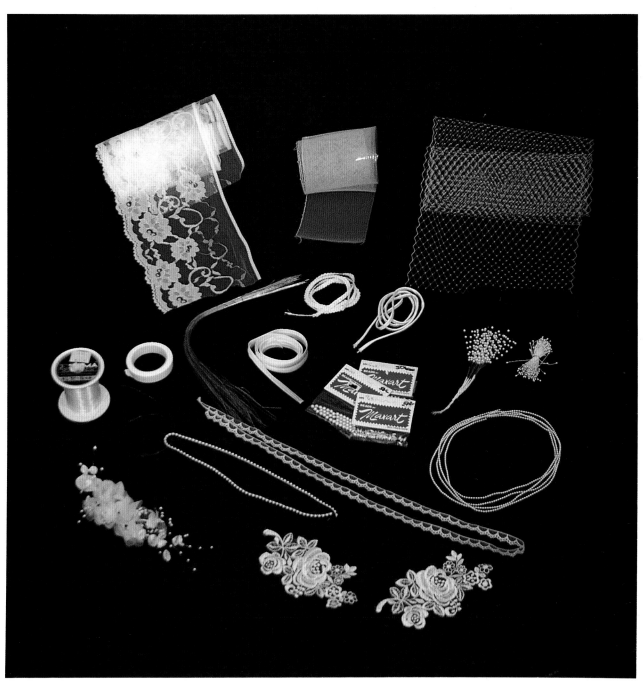

Plate 23: Materials used in making bridal trimmings and accessories
(pages 54–62)

Plate 24: Satin and sequin leaves (page 54) and fabric flowers (page 57)

Plate 25: Fabric and tulle bows (pages 58–59) and tulle ruffles (pages 59–60)

Three-Tiered Veil

Plate 21

180 cm circle with 180 × 60 cm blusher

Materials

2 metres (2¼ yds) tulle
10 metres (10½ yds) fishing line
10 metres (10½ yds) lace (optional)

Method

1. First make the finger-tip veil following previous instructions, changing the measurements of the finger-tip veil to fit in with the three-tiered veil. The finger-tip veil is still a 180 cm (71'') circle. When folding the finger-tip veil in half alter the measurements from 120 × 60 cm (47'' × 24'') to 100 × 80 cm (39'' × 31'').

BLUSHER

2. You should have 200 × 90 cm (80'' × 36'') tulle left. Lay on a flat surface and measure 180 cm (71'') along the top and 60 cm (24'') down the side. See diagram 1. Cut out.
3. Fold the tulle from left to right so it measures 90 × 60 cm (36'' × 24''), then curve the corner. See diagram 2.
4. Fold veil as in diagram 3 and gather across to measure 9 cm (3½''). Attach this to the finger-tip veil.

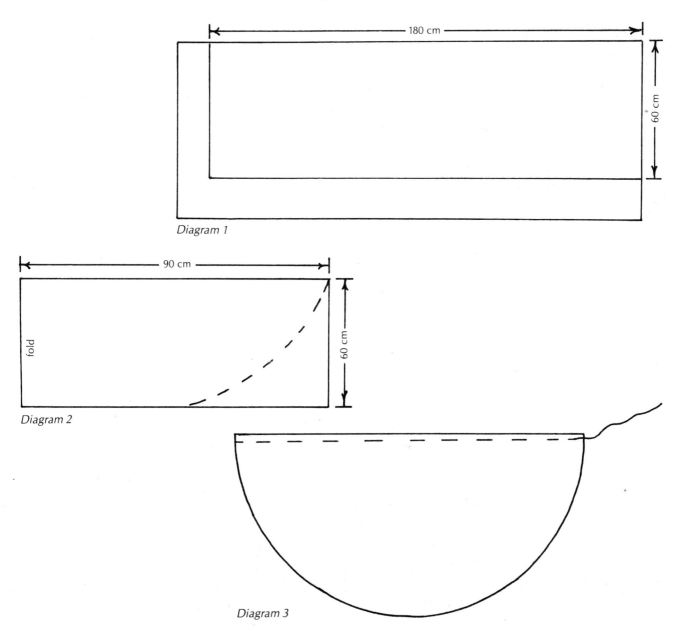

Diagram 1

Diagram 2

Diagram 3

Cathedral-Length Veil

Plate 22

Materials

3.6 metres (4 yds) tulle
12 metres (13½ yds) fishing line/lace
12 metres (13½ yds) lace (optional)

Method

1. Lay the tulle out on a flat surface and fold from left to right. It should measure 180 X 270 cm (71″ X 106″). See diagram 1.

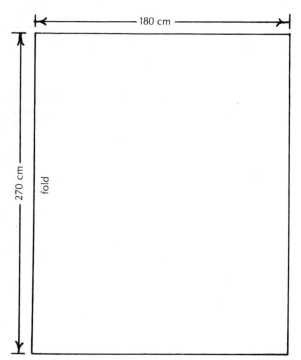

Diagram 1

2. Now fold the tulle from top to bottom so it measures 180 X 135 cm (71″ X 53″). Curve the corner as in diagram 2.

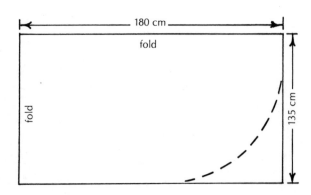

Diagram 2

3. Unfold the tulle and lay it on a flat surface. To make the blusher or face veil fold the tulle over 60 cm (24″). See diagram 3.

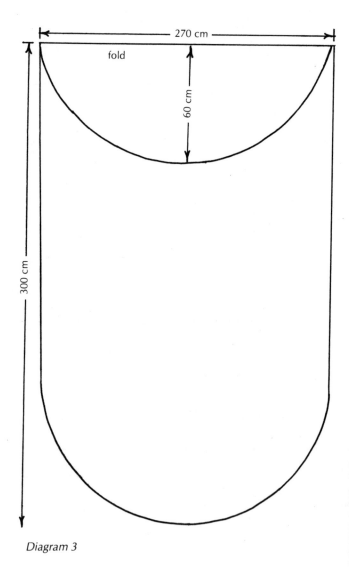

Diagram 3

4. Now gather the veil to measure 9 cm (3½''). This can be done in two ways. You can gather right across the fold line, which creates a very full veil, or you can gather just the middle section. See diagrams 4 and 5.

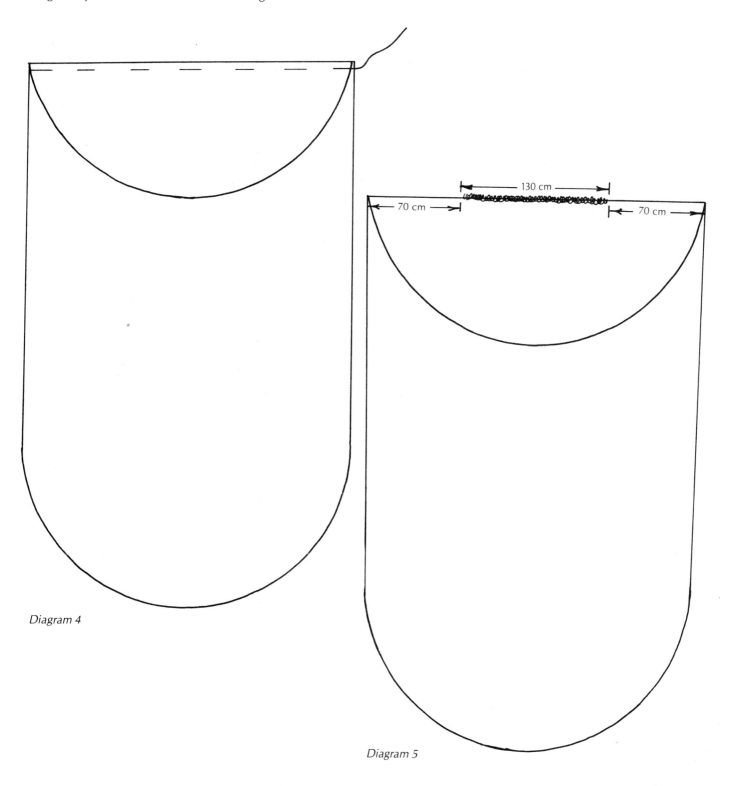

Diagram 4

130 cm

70 cm

70 cm

Diagram 5

6 Bridal Trimmings

Satin Leaves

Plate 24

Materials
25 cm (10″) satin fabric
26 gauge florist's wire
White florist's tape
Needle and cotton

Method
1. Cut a square of fabric 10 × 10 cm (4″ × 4″). Fold corner to corner to make a triangle, then fold again to make a smaller triangle.
2. Sew with running stitch along the non-folded edge. Insert a piece of wire up through the centre of the leaf, then gather the stitching up tight and twist the remaining cotton around both fabric and wire. See diagrams 1 and 2.
3. To tidy up the flower stem cut away excess fabric and bind with florist's tape.

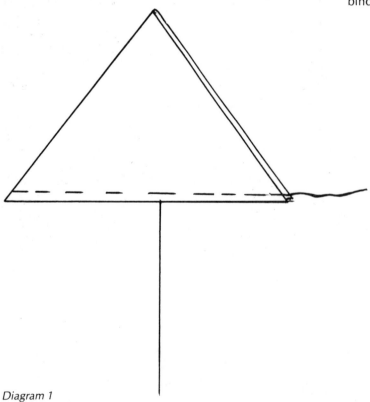

Diagram 1   Diagram 2

Plate 26: Trimming a veil with appliqué flowers (page 60)

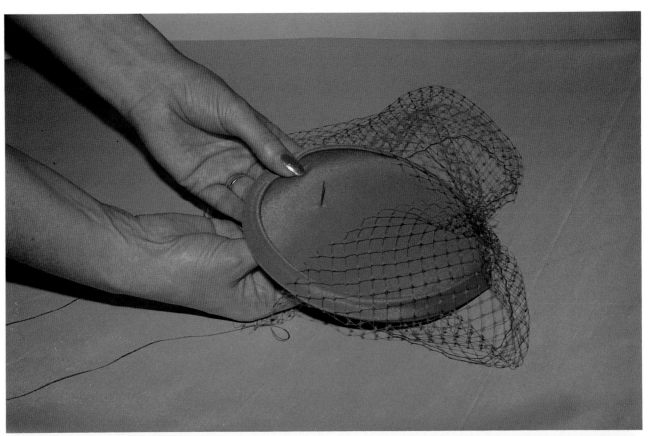

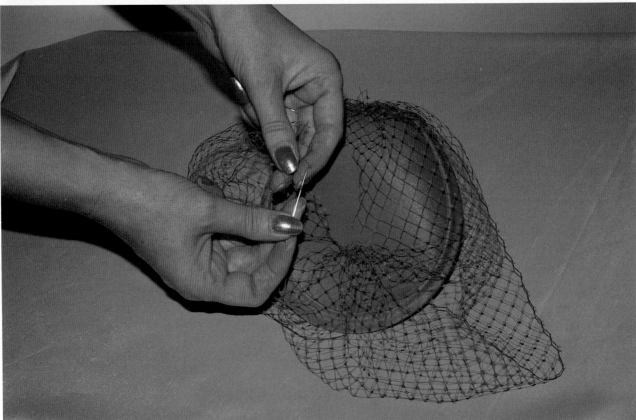

Plates 27 and 28: Steps in applying veiling to a hat (page 61)

56

Sequin Leaves

Plate 24

Materials

Nylon net leaves or millinery leaves
5 metres (5½ yds) sequins (will make 28 leaves)
Glue
Florist's tape

Method

1. Apply glue all over the leaf. Affix the sequin strip starting at the base of the leaf and working around it, finishing up in the middle. See diagrams 1 and 2.
2. Tidy up leaf stem with florist's tape.

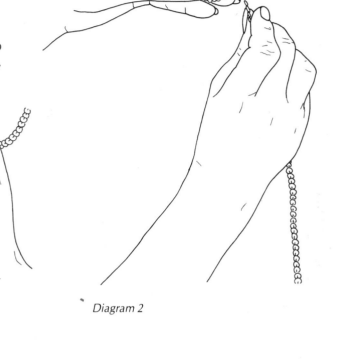

Diagram 2

Diagram 1

Fabric Flowers

Plate 24

Materials

Fabric (organza, poly satin, fine silk)
26 gauge florist's wire
Florist's tape
1 bunch of pearl stamens

Method

1. Take three stamens and fold in half. Place a piece of florist's wire against them and tape together. See diagram 1.
2. Cut fabric on the bias 25 X 10 cm (10'' X 4''), fold lengthways, curve the end, and make a running stitch from one end to the other along the unfolded edge. See diagram 2.

Diagram 1

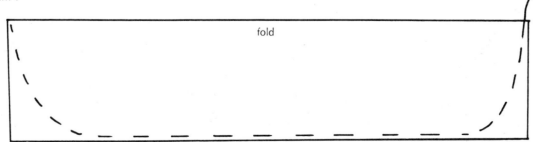

fold

Diagram 2

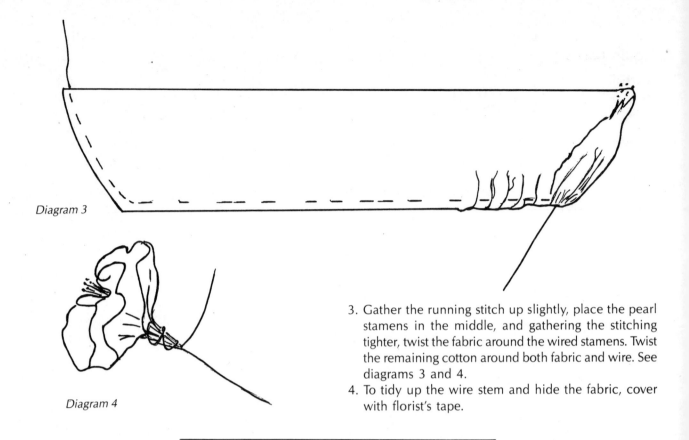

Diagram 3

Diagram 4

3. Gather the running stitch up slightly, place the pearl stamens in the middle, and gathering the stitching tighter, twist the fabric around the wired stamens. Twist the remaining cotton around both fabric and wire. See diagrams 3 and 4.
4. To tidy up the wire stem and hide the fabric, cover with florist's tape.

Fabric Bow

Plate 25

Materials
50 cm (20'') fabric
Needle and cotton

Method
1. Cut fabric to 30 × 12 cm (12'' × 5''). Fold lengthways so the raw edges meet in the centre, then press with a warm iron along the fold lines. Now take the ends and bring them into the centre. Sew with a gathering stitch, pull tight and secure. See diagrams 1 and 2.
2. To cover the centre of the bow, you need another small piece of fabric 3 × 4 cm (1¼'' × 1½''). Fold the raw edges into the centre lengthways and press with a warm iron (following the same method as above). Wrap the strip around the centre of the bow, fold one end and stitch in place. See diagram 3.

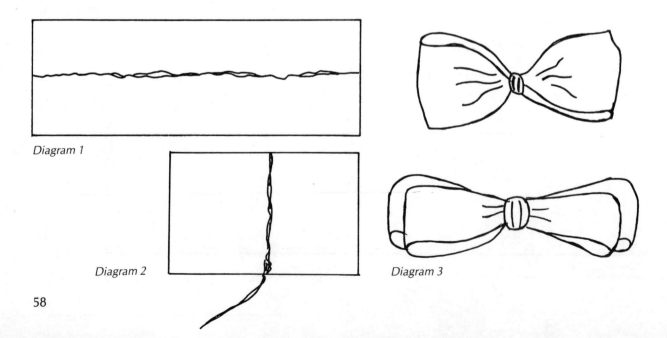

Diagram 1

Diagram 2

Diagram 3

58

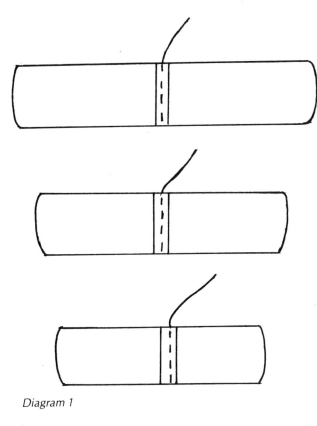

Tulle Bow

Plate 25

Materials

Tulle 180 × 20 cm (71″ × 8″)
Needle and cotton

Method

1. Cut the tulle into three pieces 70 × 20 cm, 60 × 20 cm and 50 × 20 cm (28″ × 8″, 24″ × 8″, 19″ × 8″).
2. Fold each piece of tulle separately as for the fabric bow, bringing the ends in to the centre and joining with a loose running stitch. Pull tight and secure, then layer the bows from large to small and sew these layers together. See diagrams 1 and 2.

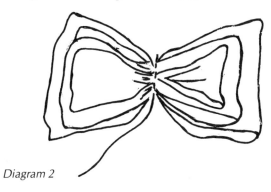

Diagram 1

Diagram 2

Tulle Ruffle 1

Plate 25

Materials

150 × 15 cm (60″ × 6″) tulle
150 cm (60″) fishing line
Needle and cotton

Method

1. Lay the tulle out on a flat surface and cut it so the ends are curved. See diagram 1.
2. Following the instructions for fluting bridal veils (see page 44), flute along the longer straight edge only.

3. Gather the tulle along the curved section and the shorter straight edge. See diagram 2.

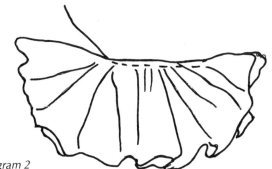

Diagram 2

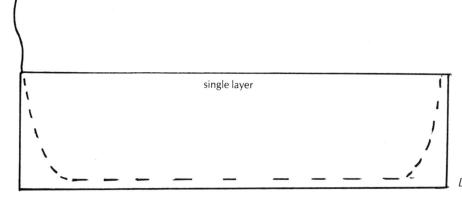

single layer

Diagram 1

Tulle Ruffle 2

Plate 25

Materials
150 × 30 cm (60″ × 12″) tulle
Needle and cotton

Method
Fold tulle in half lengthways and curve both ends. With a running stitch gather the tulle along the non-folded line and the curved edge until it measures 9 cm (3½″). See diagrams 1 and 2.

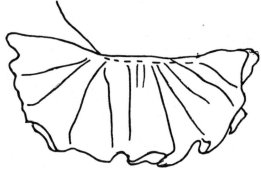

Diagram 2

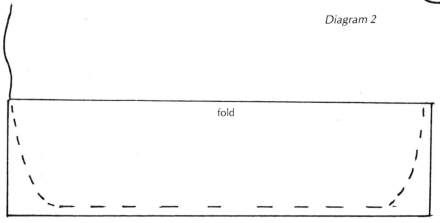

fold

Diagram 1

Trimming the Veil with Appliqué Flowers

Plate 26

Materials
Veil
10 appliqué flowers
Needle and cotton
Pins

Method
1. Arrange the appliqués on the veil, if necessary cutting them into smaller flowers to achieve a satisfactory design. The diagram shows two appliqués arranged back to back.
2. When you have decided on your design, pin all flowers and leaves in place and then tack them.
3. You can either do a fine whip stitch around each flower and leaf or a small tacking stitch in each corner of every flower and leaf.

How to Apply Veiling to Hats   *Plates 27, 28*

COCKTAIL HATS

Materials
75 cm (30'') hat veiling
Needle and cotton

Method
1. Cut a 5 cm (2'') strip lengthways from the veiling. See the diagram.

2. Gather both ends of the wider piece of veiling and sew to the back of the hat. The cut edge should be towards the top of the hat.
3. Insert the needle up through the shape about 5 cm (2'') from the front edge, and gather the excess veiling until the cut edge is taut on top of the hat. Sew and secure stitching. See plates 27 and 28 on page 56.
4. Make a bow out of the remaining veiling and sew to the back of the hat.

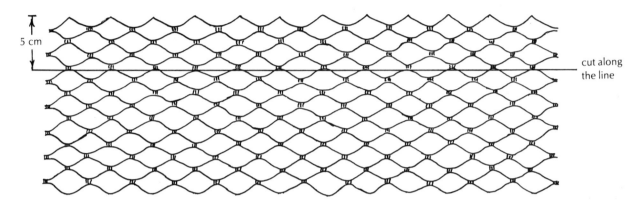

5 cm

cut along
the line

BRIM HATS

Materials
1 metre (39'') veiling
Needle and cotton

Method
1. Trim the edge of the veiling on one side only, gather both ends and sew them to the back of the hat.
2. Gather the veiling in six sections, three on each side of the hat. Starting with the two front gathers, sew just below the crown edge. See the diagram. (This method can be adapted to most cocktail hats as well.)

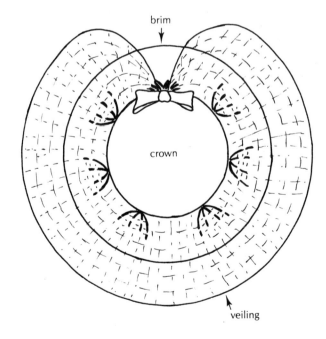

brim

crown

veiling

How to Cut Fabric on the Bias

Materials
Fabric
Dressmaking ruler
Tailor's chalk

Method
Most cocktail hats need 50 cm (20'') of fabric for their band.

1. To cut fabric on the true bias, lay it on a flat surface and measure 50 cm (20'') across the bottom and along one side. Draw a diagonal line connecting these two points. See diagram 1.

2. Measure 10 cm (4'') back from the original points on both edges. Draw another diagonal line to connect these points as well. See diagram 2. Cut out the strip.

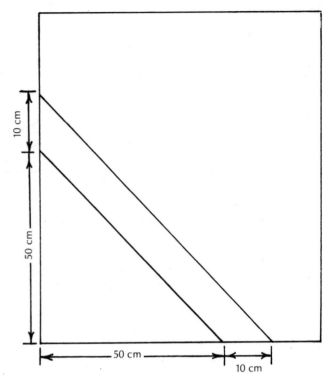

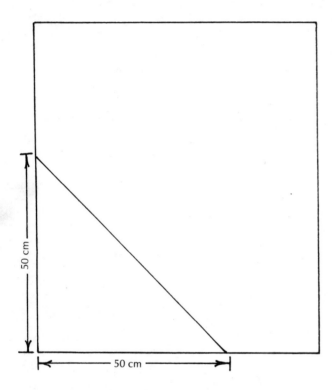

7 Blocking Your Own Shapes

There are various foundation materials on the market; the main one in use today is called leno or marli, and also 20/20. This is a fairly open-weave material and heavily starched. Other foundation materials are buckram, cap net and sparterie (willow). These are not used as much as they have become very costly. Leno is a very easy foundation material to work with as it will take a fair amount of wetting before it falls apart.

Blocking is fairly easy. If you don't possess a head block, as a temporary measure a polystyrene head will do the trick (the short-neck type). You can use elastic to hold the leno in place. Thumb tacks are too short, so use long dressmaking pins. A saucepan can be used as a stopgap block for a pill box hat.

The block should be covered with plastic wrap. Cover it about three times, continuing the wrap under the block. If only one layer is used it will have a tendency to come off every time you block; three layers stay there for quite a few blockings.

To dry foundation materials quickly, place the block in an upright drying cabinet or in front of a fan heater. Shapes usually dry in about 10 to 15 minutes.

For wiring hat shapes and brims buttonhole stitch can be used. If you are using a machine, which is faster, use zigzag stitch at the widest setting and about midway for length. Go slowly at first and with practice you will find it becomes easier, and faster.

Equipment
Plate 2

1. Millinery blocks
2. Thumb tacks
3. Foundation material (leno)
4. Millinery wire
5. 1 cm (½'') wide elastic
6. Old towel
7. Tape measure
8. Old scissors
9. Wire snips
10. Plastic wrap
11. Tailor's chalk
12. Sewing machine

Points to Remember

1. Cover the block with plastic wrap before blocking, otherwise stain from the wood will come out onto your foundation; also the foundation will stick to the block.
2. Always overlap wire 5 cm (2'') around all hat and brim shapes for added support.
3. Do not wet cap net too much as the starch will wash out.
4. Steam or slightly dampen willow only, as the cotton backing will fall away if too much water is applied.

Pear Shape

Materials
25 × 25 cm (10″ × 10″) leno
60 cm (24″) millinery wire
Tailor's chalk/HB pencil
Thumb tacks
Elastic
Head block
Old towel
Tape measure

Method
1. Wet the leno, then place it on a towel to remove excess water.
2. Place the leno over the prepared block, with the corners facing the back, front and sides. This gives maximum stretch.
3. Stretch the leno over the block, placing the elastic around it. Keep stretching the leno to eliminate any wrinkles. Now place thumb tacks through the elastic into the leno at the back, front and sides. See diagram 1.

4. To eliminate any stubborn wrinkles, pull the leno, at the same time inserting a few more tacks below the elastic.
5. Leave the leno on the block until it is thoroughly dry.
6. Measurements for the pear shape are: front to back 20 cm (8″), side to side 16 cm (6½″), across the back 8 cm (3″).
7. Mark the centre with tailor's chalk. Measure from the centre to the front 10 cm (4″), then from the centre to the back 10 cm (4″), from the centre to both sides 8 cm (3″), also to side front points and side back points 9 cm (3½″). Draw a line measuring 8 cm (3″) across the back. See diagram 2.

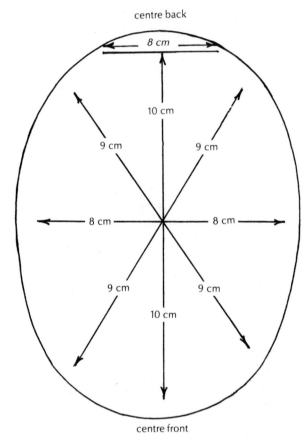

Diagram 2

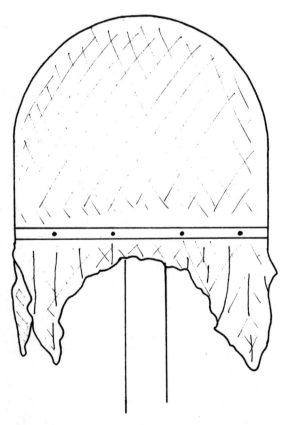

Diagram 1

8. With chalk or a light pencil now shape the hat. See diagram 3.
9. Remove the leno from the block, cut out the shape and wire the edge.

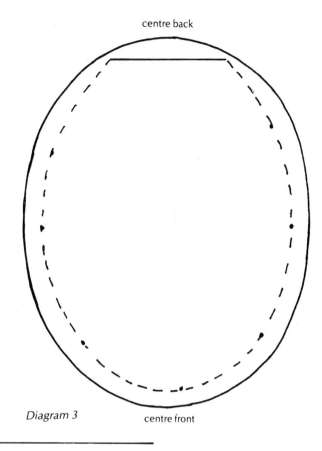

Diagram 3

Pearl Shape

Materials
25 × 25 cm (10″ × 10″) leno
60 cm (24″) millinery wire
Tailor's chalk/HB pencil
Elastic
Head block
Thumb tacks
Old towel
Tape measure

Method
1. Follow the basic instructions for the pear shape.
2. Measurements are: front to back, 22 cm (9″), side to side, 18 cm (7″), centre to side front points 9.5 cm (3¾″), and centre to side back points 10 cm (4″). Mark these with chalk, shaping the centre front into a point.
3. Remove the leno from the block, cut the shape out and wire the edge. See diagram.

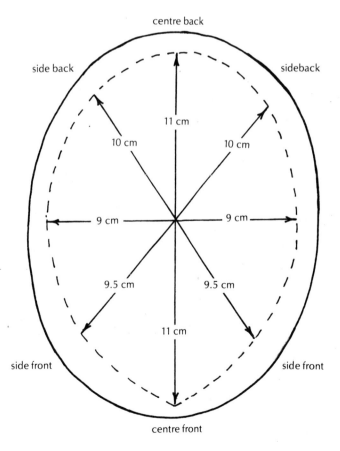

Pill Box Shape

Materials

25 × 25 cm (10″ × 10″) leno
60 cm (24″) millinery wire
Tailor's chalk/HB pencil
Thumb tacks
Elastic
Pill box head block
Old towel
Tape measure

Method

1. Follow the basic instructions for blocking the pear shape.
2. Measurements will be determined by your own pill box block.
3. When the leno is dry measure down and mark with chalk 5 cm (2″) at the back, front and side points, remove from block and cut shape out. Wire the edge. See diagram.

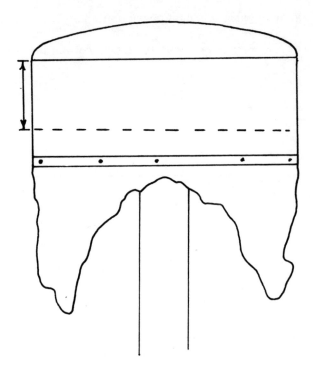

Shallow Crown

Materials

30 × 30 cm (12″ × 12″) leno
60 cm (24″) millinery wire
Tailor's chalk/HB pencil
Elastic
Head block
Thumb tacks
Old towel
Tape measure

Method

1. Follow the instructions for blocking the pear shape. Crown measurements are 22 × 20 cm (8½″ × 8″).
2. Find the centre of the crown and measure from the centre to the front 11 cm (4½″), from the centre to the back 11 cm (4½″), from the centre to each side 10 cm (4″), and from the centre to the side front and side back 10.5 cm (4¼″). Mark these points with chalk, remove the leno from the block and cut the shape out. Wire the edge. See diagram.

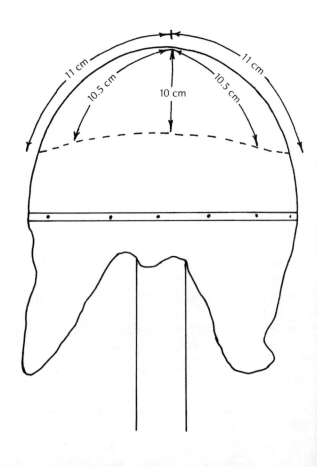

Brim Shape

Materials

35 × 35 cm (14″ × 14″) leno
1 metre (39″) millinery wire
Head block
Tape measure
Tailor's chalk/HB pencil

Method

1. Place the block on the leno and draw around it. Make an inner circle by measuring 2.5 cm (1″) into the circle at eight points. See diagram 1. Cut the inner circle out.
2. Cut the remaining leno inside the outer circle into 28 sections or tabs, each of these tabs being 2 cm (¾″) wide. See diagram 2.
3. This particular brim will be 8 cm (3″) from the collar edge. Measure out from the collar area 8 cm (3″) at 16 points, then pencil around to make the shape. See diagrams 3 and 4. Cut out the shape and wire the edge.

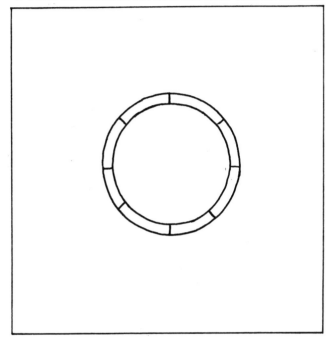

Diagram 1

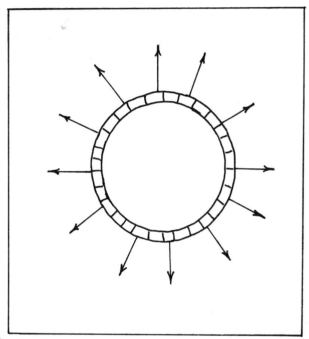

Diagram 3

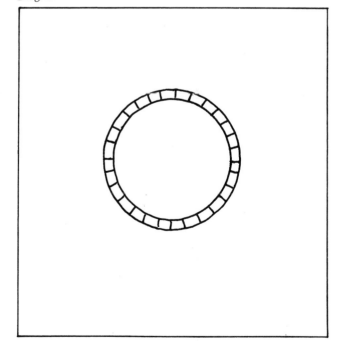

Diagram 2

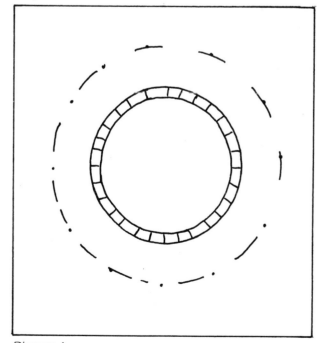

Diagram 4

Suppliers

S.A. Brown Pty Ltd
52 Shepherd Street (off Broadway)
Chippendale NSW 2008
Phone (02) 699 7343

Cyril J. Preston Pty Ltd
258 Flinders Lane
Melbourne Vic 3000
Phone (03) 654 7062

Millinery Warehouse
94 Welsby Place
New Farm Qld 4005
Phone (07) 358 3511

Homework Handicraft
17 McBean Avenue
Holden Hill SA 5088
Phone (08) 261 6401

Knit Fabric & Yards
1015 Lower North East Rd
Highbury SA 5089
Phone (08) 264 5119

Meg Sheen Craftsmans Suppliers
308 Hay Street
Subiaco WA 6008
Phone (09) 381 8215

Gilberts Bridal and Floral Handcrafts
306 Murray Street (basement level)
Perth WA 6000
Phone (09) 321 9873

Many department and craft stores carry millinery supplies.

Index